Discover Mammals

by Amanda Trane

© 2017 by Amanda Trane
ISBN: 9781532402654
eISBN: 9781532402661
Images licensed from Fotolia.com
All rights reserved.
No portion of this book may be reproduced
without express permission of the publisher.
First Edition
Published in the United States by
Xist Publishing
www.xistpublishing.com
PO Box 61593 Irvine, CA 92602

When you look at an animal, can you tell if it is a mammal? This fox is a mammal.

Some people think that all mammals have paws or hands. This is not true! This Caribou has hooves and it is a mammal.

5

Some people think that mammals do not lay eggs. It is true that birds, fish, and lizards are not mammals, but there are special mammals that do lay eggs.
This platypus lays eggs.

Some people think that all mammals live on land. This is not true! You can also look for mammals in rivers and in the ocean. This whale is a mammal.

All mammals have three things in common. All mammals are warm-blooded, have fur, and drink milk. This mountain goat is a mammal.

11

All mammals are warm-blooded. That means the temperature of their blood stays about the same, even if it is a hot day or it is snowing outside. This elk keeps his blood the same temperature even when it is below freezing outside.

13

Polar bears swim in the icy ocean but they keep their blood the same temperature as human beings. When they get too hot, they swim in cold water to cool down.

This dog is warm-blooded. He can only sweat on his feet and his nose, so he opens his mouth and breaths in and out to help cool down. This is called panting.

Bears are warm-blooded but their blood changes temperature when they hibernate. When a bear sleeps through the winter, his blood temperature goes down.

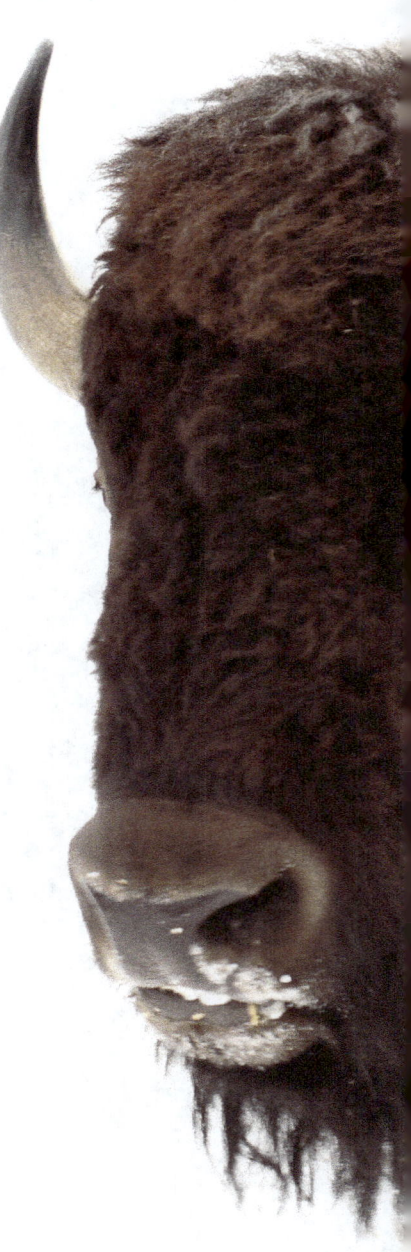

All mammals have fur or hair. This bison has thick outer hair and a soft downy undercoat. Bison down can be made into yarn.

22

This wild boar has thick, rough hair. The hair or bristles of a wild boar can be used to make a hairbrush.

Even mammals in the ocean have hair. When a dolphin is born it has tiny hairs that fall out as it grows up.

All mammals feed their babies milk. This fox cub will drink milk from her mother for about two months.

This fawn needs to drink milk for about 4 months. After two months, he will start to eat leaves and grass, but he still needs milk to grow strong.

Some mammals need to drink milk for a long time. A baby blue whale drinks up to 200 liters per day for at least 6 months.

If you are not sure if something is a mammal, ask three questions. Is it warm-blooded? Does it have hair? Does it drink milk? If you answer, 'yes' to all three questions, it is a mammal!

www.ingramcontent.com/pod-product-compliance
Lightning Source LLC
LaVergne TN
LVHW021601070426
835507LV00014B/1890